WHISPER ON THE SHORE

*Dedicated to my wife
and our family and friends
with love*

WHISPER ON THE SHORE

Peter Burgham

Copyright © Peter Burgham 2020

The right of Peter Burgham to be identified as the author of this book has been asserted in accordance with the Copyright, Designs and Patents Act 1988.

First Printing: 2020

Minor errata: 2023

ISBN 978-1-9163353-4-9   (paperback)

All rights reserved. No part of this publication may be reproduced, stored in a retrieval system, or transmitted, at any time or by any means (electronic, mechanical, photocopying, recording, or otherwise) without the prior written permission of the publisher.

Published by: Peter Burgham
                York, England

A CIP catalogue record for this book is available from the British Library.

Website: www.burg34.com

Cover image: Lake Geneva sunset

Contents

The Colour of Music 7
Silvio's 8
Song for a Rainy Day 9
Sea View Guaranteed 10
Wrong Number 11
Say it with Flowers 12
Business Trip to the Coast 12
Keeping it Fresh 12
Cut to the Heart 13
Without You 14
Tying the Knot at Gretna 15
Heartbeat of Youth 16
Whisper It Softly 17
Love Boat 20
Coastal Erosion 20
Simmering Point 21
Business As Usual 22
Yorkshire Life 23
On Nights Like These 24
Secret of the Glen 26
Burning Sky 27

The Colour of Music

I see music in the simple things: a vase,
a pen, a flower; a symphony in this palette
of paints, a concerto in these rain-
spattered windows; an opera in your eyes.

I hear a cascade of colours
in the sunlight of your smile, the whirl
of Danube blue, the swirl of peacock
green, the clamour of cotton white.

I see the Memphis in your lips, the Motown
in your hips, I hear the cocktail of Manhattan,
the sapphire and flamenco red,
the rainbow jazz progression.

You are my beat, my rhythm, my rhapsody,
my rondo, my nocturne and my polka,
my *chanson d'amour*, my *leitmotif*,
my favourite moonlight sonata.

Chords of light from simple things: these pink
flowers gift-wrapped on the table, the pen
that signs with love this valentine card,
this little ensemble, this perfect *étude en rose*.

Silvio's

Those days you could make it
we sailed with the wind,
parties, nightclubs, candlelit table
at the marina bistro.

They knew us well at Silvio's,
we'd order romance *à la carte*
to a serenade of Dean Martin
and waiters singing *That's Amore*.

Yachts bobbing in the amber
sunset, the harbour breeze
strumming the mast rigs
like guitar strings.

Walking close to the edge
we'd hoist flags, ponder
our chances of falling
headlong into our own reflections.

Those days you could make it,
those were the days.

Song for a Rainy Day

We kissed in the rain
we laughed, we ran
we hugged, held hands
we had no plan.

Thirty years ago
young lovers
catching raindrops
between our tingling lips.

I wonder
are you out there
somewhere
catching raindrops
still
tingling in the rain ?

Just tingling in the rain
what a glorious feeling
what a happy ...

I know, I know
showing my age
but couldn't resist.

Miss you sometimes
like today
in this unseasonal
tingling mist.

Sea View Guaranteed

A stone's throw from the sea
fully air-conditioned, rated
off the chart, a billion stars

bodies berthed on beds
of fine white sand
no checkout time

a breath of salt air & seaweed
the dawn craik of gulls
eager for crab and fish

waves unfurl their tongues
and kiss the shoreline
with gentle surf

we sip the cocktail
breathe the light
raise the mainsail

choose our course
leave city stripes
behind closed doors.

Wrong Number

She gave me the wrong number,
the girl who answered
the door of flat 3A
where you used to live
and we used to kiss
and fumble the nights away.

Remember how we'd dance
in the candlelight
by the moon-caressed sill
(you never did pay
your electricity bill).

Is it really a year ago
since we last talked,
if talk is what you'd call it,
it's the talk that got in the way,
the words that went
and spoiled it.

I tried to phone you today,
but got some angry guy,
said he knew my name,
knew where I lived.

Seems like the world
is getting smaller,
but that's no consolation
to the long-distance
midnight caller.

Say it with Flowers

On impulse I bought you flowers, cut,
Chrysanthemums, yellow, and rudbeckia, red,
Some in bloom, some in bud,
Guaranteed for a week, it said.

Flowers that were fit for a beautiful princess,
A bunch of the best, the pick of the crop,
But if I thought it would guarantee your happiness,
My petal, I'd buy you the whole bloomin' shop.

Business Trip to the Coast

Lovely breakfast, lovely view,
but nowhere near as lovely
as breakfast in bed with you.

Keeping it Fresh

Consider the blackberry
but try not to do it
like every other
Tom, Jack and Jerry.

Cut to the Heart

I nearly missed the point today
- it'll come as no surprise -
Those short green stems that you laid
Quietly on the desk meant nothing in my eyes.

Plastic or real ? I couldn't tell.
Odd act, but not enough to distract from my literary
Endeavours - which had been going well -
I typed on, sure you would elaborate if necessary.

"They've been neatly cut," you finally said.
No incision yet into my thinking.
"They were carnations, white, pink, and red."
You looked at me without blinking.

At this, I sympathised, "What a shame, such a lovely flower."
But still not reading the look you gave,
Until you answered with a disconsolate glower,
"Yesterday, I put them on my father's grave."

Ah, the dawning; but I'm glad I refrained from asking,
Why you'd laid those short green stems at the graveside,
For now I could sense the hurt you were masking,
And so a comforting hug for a heart opened wide:

"People can be cruel, I know that's nothing new,
But no matter if they think they're smart,
Don't let them change the things you do,
My floribunda rose, my very dearest heart."

Without You

I'd be

<table>
<tr><td>

a bird
without
  a wing

a hive
without
  a bee

a train
without
  a track

a boat
without
  a tiller

a piper
without
  a tune

a torch
without
  a light

a diary
without
  a date

a thorn
without
  a rose

</td><td>

a bell
without
  a ring

a lock
without
  a key

a front
without
  a back

a bridge
without
  a pillar

a desert
without
  a dune

a left
without
  a right

a soul
without
  a mate

a writer
without
  a close

</td></tr>
</table>

Tying the Knot at Gretna

Estuary of legend the Solway Firth,
distant ships cutting a steady wake
towards the setting sun,
stowaways breathless in anticipation
amongst the trappings and the rigs,
catching the promise of epic skies,
fires burning and full steam ahead
over the marital horizon.

Go bravely rose-tinted runaways
heed the auguries of the sea
respect the storm and the calm
and though flat-broke before the knot
you shall ever be the richer
when you reach your final spot.

Heartbeat of Youth

The most important people in your life
Are those you've yet to meet,
You'll know them when you see them,
Your heart will miss a beat.

But in that fractured second,
Hold heaven if you dare,
If not, be warned, your heart may break
Beyond all earth's repair.

Whisper It Softly

        Soaring like a sea-bird
        on a coastal breeze
        above the island

the sky was paradise-blue
the sails of yachts billowed
    golden-yellow

the kiss on the beach
she thought would last forever
like the name she'd drawn in the sand.

Telling her softly	on the crest of her dream
Telling her softly	like a babbling stream
Telling her softly	what she's longing to hear
Telling her softly	that the wedding was near
Telling her softly	

    The soft peal of bells
      stroked her face
    with gossamer silk

the sky was bone-white
her wedding-dress billowed
and danced with the clouds

the kiss in the church
she thought would last forever
like the name she'd signed in permanent blue.

Holding her gently	in the tender moonlight
Holding her gently	till deep in the night
Holding her gently	with the promise of more
Holding her gently	behind the closed door
Holding her gently	

       They decorated the apartment
           to minimalist design
            in shades of beige

        the sky was functional blue
              jet trails faded
             into the distance

          the kiss in the bedroom
         she thought would last forever
      like the perfume he'd draped on her neck.

Softly he wandered   down an unmarked track
Softly he wandered   and didn't look back
Softly he wandered   inside a dark cloud
Softly he wandered   away from the crowd
Softly he wandered

             Startled as a deer
          running through a forest
       she breathed deep the oak-wood

            under a canopy of grey
          the sunlight came scarce
         through the pockets of mist

             the kiss in the rain
        she'd thought would last forever
      like a flower picked fresh from the bed.

Breaking it gently   that he'd heard a new voice
Breaking it gently   when she gave him a choice
Breaking it gently   when she opened her heart
Breaking it gently   when they're falling apart
Breaking it gently

        Trapped like a bear
          on an arctic floe
  drifting through storm-black days

      she made ice-sculptures
       in unvisited ice-parks
   and roamed her ice kingdom

       the kiss in the dark
   she'd thought would last forever
like footprints trailing crisp in the snow.

Whisper it softly	he struck a new pose
Whisper it softly	he offered a rose
Whisper it softly	they held hands again
Whisper it softly	they kissed in the rain
Whisper it softly	

Love Boat

Time goes slowly
on a desert island
for the stranded voyager
watching bananas ripen
in the midday sun
missing the passing ship.

Coastal Erosion

Invisibly hewn by rock gnawing rock,
Washed away to unknown shores,
Tearing at the skin of the land,
Beaten by the relentless waves,
Bowed by the pressing of the wind.

As the parting sun bestowed its crown
On the rim of the majestic stack,
In the heat of cancerian June,
She stood alone on the beach,
Listening to the ocean, anchored to the moon.

Simmering Point

It's all about the custard, that Roman wife
hitting upon a fluke of eggs, sugar, milk,
cornflour and vanilla pod, weighing the odds
of filling the bowl to perfection.

Mixing to the rhythm of the spatula beat
from the Latin meaning broad blade,
blender-in-chief, whisk-me-away to
the olive groves of perfect confection.

Avoiding the issues formed by skin,
no trifle to avoid the curdle,
bringing it to the simmering point,
keeping the lid on careless convection.

Knowing the moment to turn down the heat
and never shy of putting a fancy name to it
from *crème pâtissière* to *crème anglaise*
whatever the simplicity of its complexion.

It's all about the custard, the perfect Roman
accompaniment to the roasted parrot,
pickled mice or ostrich pie, a dessert
fit for even the emperor's inspection.

Business As Usual

What were the odds ? Spain wasn't it ?
He saw her first, stepped forward, polite,
civilised, charming as ever.

They couldn't believe it, had it really been that long ?
They'd both moved on, of course, down different paths,
formed new and imperfect circles of friends and lovers.

They talked over dinner at the casino,
Sardinian *fregola, zabaione, rosé di Alghero*,
stood on the terrace and watched the fireworks display

above the harbour: cascades, serpents, Chinese
rockets dancing in the moonlight, reflections glinting
on the water, memories of their old romance.

She said she had to leave, Morocco, business.
They exchanged phone numbers. He went back
to his world of import/export.

It was several months later he heard her name,
on the TV News, her body washed up on the shore
identified only by her red dragon tattoo.

The filmclips flashed by: Hong Kong, the skin on his back
etched by her nails, those hot nights in Malaga,
how she always made an excuse to leave early,

the way she would describe her husband's yacht
as a floating prison. He remembered with affection
her tendency to dramatise.

Smiling ironically he lit the fuse with his cigar, dived
overboard in his wetsuit, and nonchalantly ignoring
the debris and the sharks, swam strongly ashore.

*

Alone on the sofa, his snoring jolted into his midnight swim.
He slouched across to the kitchen past the empty crisp bags,
crushed cans and tattoo parlour leaflets, and dived into the
fridge for another Red Dragon beer.

Yorkshire Life

Yorkshire Thrift
Roses are white
Brambles are black
I'll give thee a kiss
But tha'll owe me one back.

Yorkshire Pride
Roses are white
Bluebells are blue
If it's good enough for Yorkshire
It's good enough for you.

Yorkshire Logic
Roses are white
Bluebells are pink
'Appen that's not
As daft as tha'd think.

Yorkshire Opinion
Roses are white
Pansies are blue
If I want your opinion
I'll give it to you.

Yorkshire Cuisine
Roses are red
Violets are blue
We love all the Yonners
But they're reet hard to chew.

** *Yonner* is used here to mean broadly 'Lancastrian'.

On Nights Like These

In the room full of strangers
all the faces seemed
strangely familiar.

The couples dancing,
shuffling their untrained feet
to the rhythm of the safe old beat

routinely played out
by the spangle-suited band
who'd long ago lost count

of the spangle-headed girls
they'd banged in the back of the van
on nights like these.

The raucous laughter at the bar,
back-slapping, ale-quaffing,
wench-grabbing, like their fathers,

grandfathers, and mediaeval
forefathers with uncanny resemblance
in this place before.

The pot-belly dreamer
at the fat-chance saloon
besotted by the hypnotic

bare midriffs
of the unattainable
slim dancers.

The faded queen of the night
with fag and gin
sitting engrossed in talk

with her former self,
indulging in a journey
of more exotic origin.

The conga round the floor
past the congratulations banner,
examining every link in the chain,

odd no sign yet of Bob and Jane,
so once more to the bar, beer friends,
as you do on nights like these,

take a double, save the queue,
another double-take, the bride
a stranger too.

Asked the barman, is there another
Plaza Hotel ? Only one Plaza pal,
and busy tonight, what with the other wedding

upstairs as well. Ah... still, glad I came,
enjoyed the buffet, the cabaret too,
and the band wasn't bad either,

even if the nostalgia
was wearing a bit thin,
but look it's getting late,

so tell me all
about yourself, darlin',
can I get you another gin ?

Secret of the Glen

At the ceilidh of the Invisibles, Love is in the Air. Magic and Magnetism dance a reel with Liberty and Frivolity. Mystery and Fun strip the willow with Energy, and even Dignity joins in. Gravity falls for Levity. The elders, Tolerance and Patience, watch quietly from the sides.

But the uninvited, the outcast gang: Power, Hate, Envy, Anger, Greed, Inequality and their cronies, wearing jackets emblazoned 'The Fear', snarl their motorbikes onto the dancefloor, scattering Faith, Hope and Charity. The din is deafening, silencing Music, leaving Happiness in tears.

Love despairs, but Action steps forward with Imagination to organise a circle with Defiance, Resilience and Fortitude, coaxing Doubt and the others to join. Holding hands they advance together, surrounding The Fear, chanting in unison, making themselves heard and visible. Fear has no answer.

The Invisibles are back home in the glen now, going about their daily chores, but they know that there may always come a Time when they will need once more to be Visible. Time agrees. Watch me, he says, slipping away.

Burning Sky

What snaps the bough
What fans the flame
What wrecks the home
Who plays this game

Who kindled the fire
Who laid down the stake
Who wins the top prize
What news isn't fake

What climate change
What ozone gap
What forest loss
Who burns the map

Who kindled the fire
Who laid down the stake
Who wins the top prize
What news isn't fake

Why the heartless denial
Why the obvious lie
Why no credible action
Why risk this burning sky ?

ACKNOWLEDGEMENTS

Also by the same author:

BIRD'S EYE VIEW

TRIBUTE NIGHT AT THE SOCIAL

PAUSE AND REWIND *(series)*

TOUCHPOINTS

CONNECTIONS

More poetry and verse and links to other creative arts can be found on:

www.burg34.com

Note:
Any similarity to any real persons or locations or products would be coincidental.

www.ingramcontent.com/pod-product-compliance
Lightning Source LLC
Chambersburg PA
CBHW071759080526
44588CB00013B/2306